Tom's train ride

Story by Jenny Giles

Illustrations by Chantal Stewart

One day,
Tom and his mother
went to a park.

"Look, Mom," said Tom.
"I can see some children
having a ride on a little train."

Tom and Mom went over
to the fence.

The children waved to Tom,
and he waved back.

"They are having a good ride,"
said Tom.
"But I can't go on that train.
I can't sit in it by myself."

Tom said, "Look, Mom!
I can see a wheelchair.
One of the children at the park
has a wheelchair, too!"

Then Tom saw a yellow train.
"A girl is sitting in a big seat
at the back of the train,"
he said.

The children got off the train.

But the girl stayed in the seat.

Then her father helped her

get into the wheelchair.

The girl looked at Tom.

"Hello," she said.

"You can have a ride on this train.

It's a good train.

You can sit in the big seat."

Tom sat in the seat
at the back of the train.

Toot-toot!

The train went into a tunnel.

Toot-toot!

It came out again.

Tom waved to Mom
and the girl.
"I'm having fun on this train!"
he said.